GETTING TO KI
THE U.S. PRESIDENTS

B I L L
CLINTON

FORTY-SECOND PRESIDENT
1993 – 2001

WRITTEN AND ILLUSTRATED BY MIKE VENEZIA

CHILDREN'S PRESS
AN IMPRINT OF SCHOLASTIC INC.
NEW YORK   TORONTO   LONDON   AUCKLAND   SYDNEY
MEXICO CITY   NEW DELHI   HONG KONG
DANBURY, CONNECTICUT

Reading Consultant: Nanci R. Vargus, Ed.D., Assistant Professor, School of Education, University of Indianapolis

Historical Consultant: Marc J. Selverstone, Ph.D., Assistant Professor, Miller Center of Public Affairs, University of Virginia

Photographs © 2008: AP Images: 27 (John Duricka), 25, 31 (Greg Gibson), 24 (Steve Helber), 4 (Reed Saxon); Corbis Images: 32 (Pawel Kopczynaki/Reuters), 3 (Peter Turnley), 12; Folio, Inc./Jeff Mitchell: 6; Getty Images: 7 (Luke Frazza/AFP), 16 (Bernard Gotfryd), 19 (Dirck Halstead); William J. Clinton Presidential Library: 11 (William J. Clinton Family Photographs), 8, 15, 20, 21.

Colorist for illustrations: Andrew Day

Library of Congress Cataloging-in-Publication Data

Venezia, Mike.
  Bill Clinton / written and illustrated by Mike Venezia.
    p. cm. — (Getting to know the U.S. presidents)
  ISBN-13: 978-0-516-22646-0 (lib. bdg.)   978-0-516-25460-9 (pbk.)
  ISBN-10: 0-516-22646-0 (lib. bdg.)   0-516-25460-X (pbk.)
  1. Clinton, Bill, 1946—Juvenile literature. 2. Presidents—United
States—Biography—Juvenile literature. I. Title.
  E886.V46 2008
  973.929092—dc22
  [B]
                                    2006102929

President Bill Clinton

William Jefferson Clinton, the forty-second president of the United States, was born on August 19, 1946, in Hope, Arkansas. Even at a very early age, Bill Clinton decided it was important for him to be a good citizen. He really wanted to make his community and country a better place to live.

In 1992, Arkansas governor Bill Clinton, who was running for U.S. president, played his saxophone on the *Arsenio Hall Show*.

Bill Clinton was one of the smartest men to serve as president. Bill wasn't only smart; he was pretty cool, too. When he was running for president, Bill actually played his saxophone on a popular TV show.

In 1992, Bill ran for president against President George H.W. Bush. President Bush liked things pretty much just the way they were. He appeared to be out of touch with the problems of many voters. Because Bill Clinton seemed like he could offer a fresh new start for many Americans, he won the election.

One of the problems Bill Clinton promised to fix was the economy. Prices in the United States had been going up on everything. Many people were out of work, and the U.S. government was spending a lot more money than it took in. This overspending created what is called a budget deficit.

The jobless rate in the United States was high when President Clinton took office in 1993.

During his State of the Union Address in 1999, President Clinton proudly reported how much the economy had improved during his years as president.

As president, Bill Clinton cut back on government spending and created new jobs. The economy improved. In fact, Bill Clinton oversaw the longest peacetime economic expansion in the nation's history. Before his second term as president ended, though, President Clinton was involved in a scandal that almost caused him to lose his own very important job.

Bill Clinton was originally named William Blythe III. His father, William Blythe II, died in a car accident just a few months before Bill was born. Bill took the name of his stepfather, Roger Clinton. Roger married Bill's mother, Virginia, when Bill was four years old. Roger Clinton was a car salesman.

Bill Clinton as a teenager with his mother Virginia and younger brother Roger Jr.

Unfortunately, Roger also had a drinking problem. At times, after drinking too much alcohol, Roger became violent. Bill Clinton tried to hide his family's problems. He appeared happy to his teachers and friends, and he worked hard not to let other people discover his pain.

Bill Clinton was an excellent student. The only problem his teachers had with him was when he shouted out answers before other kids could even raise their hands.

One of Bill's favorite things to do when he was little was to play in his grandfather's grocery store. At that time, Arkansas was like other segregated southern states. It had laws separating whites from blacks. Bill's grandfather didn't care about segregation, though. He treated his African-American customers the same as white customers. Bill could never understand why there were laws to keep people apart.

Bill Clinton's grandfather (right), shown here in his store, taught Bill not to judge people by the color of their skin.

Hot Springs, Arkansas, in the 1950s

When Bill was seven years old, his stepfather decided to move from Hope to the big city of Hot Springs, Arkansas. Bill continued to be a brilliant student in school. People said he always seemed more grown-up than other kids his age.

When Bill was ten, the Clintons got their first black-and-white TV set. Bill enjoyed watching the 1956 national political conventions. He was fascinated to learn how elections and politics worked. Even at such a young age, he understood what was going on.

In high school, Bill Clinton joined all kinds of organizations. He loved playing the saxophone in the school band, and he was elected class president. One of the clubs Bill joined was a political organization that sent top students to Washington, D.C., to learn about the U.S. government. On that trip to Washington, Bill Clinton's life changed forever. He got to shake hands with his hero, President John F. Kennedy! Suddenly Bill knew what he would do with his life. He would become a politician.

Sixteen-year-old Bill Clinton meets President John F. Kennedy in 1963.

After high school, Bill Clinton attended Georgetown University in Washington, D.C. He chose that school because it was located in the nation's capital. To help pay for college, Bill got a job working in the office of Arkansas Senator William Fulbright. Senator Fulbright was known for his stand against U.S. involvement in the raging war in Vietnam. Bill began to form his own antiwar feelings. Many students around the country joined in protests against the war at this time.

Students protesting against the war in Vietnam in 1969

Bill was such a good student that he was offered a Rhodes scholarship to study at Oxford University in England. Every year, only thirty-two of America's brainiest students are offered the chance to study at this fine university. Many of the Rhodes scholars Bill met became his lifelong friends. Even though Bill was very smart, he was amazed by how brilliant his classmates were.

Bill spent two years in England before
returning home. He then went to Yale Law
School. It was at Yale that Bill met the love of
his life, Hillary Rodham. One day, in the school
library, Hillary noticed that Bill kept staring at
her from across the room.

She finally went up to him and insisted they introduce themselves. Bill was happy to learn that Hillary was interested in politics, too. Soon, Bill and Hillary were inseparable. They worked together to help their favorite politicians get elected and helped each other's careers. Bill and Hillary got married in 1975. They had one daughter, Chelsea, in 1980.

Hillary, Bill, and Chelsea Clinton

Bill Clinton campaigning for Congress in 1974

Just before Bill and Hillary got married, Bill began his political career. He ran for a seat in the U.S. House of Representatives. Although Bill lost that election, he wasn't discouraged. He had learned a lot about campaigning. Next, Bill ran for attorney general of Arkansas. This time he won. Bill was now the state's top law-enforcement official.

Two years later, in 1978, Bill was encouraged to run for governor of his state. He worked harder than ever, talking to voters day and night. His hard work paid off. Bill won the election and became governor of Arkansas. At thirty-two, he was one of the youngest governors in U.S. history.

Bill Clinton is sworn in as governor of Arkansas in 1979.

Governor Clinton worked hard to improve his state's public schools. At that time, Arkansas had the poorest schools in the country. Teachers were often underpaid and some of them needed

more training. Buildings needed repair, and many students dropped out of school as soon as they could.

Right away, Governor Clinton convinced people how important education was to the future of Arkansas. He raised taxes, and appointed Hillary to head up a special committee to improve education. Governor Clinton raised money to repair badly run-down roads. He also helped create jobs for minorities and poor people. Soon, Bill Clinton began to get national attention for being one of the best governors in the country.

President George Bush (left), Ross Perot (center), and Bill Clinton debated each other on TV during the 1992 presidential campaign.

In 1992, the Democratic Party chose Bill Clinton to run for president against Republican President George H.W. Bush. The Republican and Democratic parties are the biggest political organizations in the United States. But a wealthy businessman named Ross Perot joined the race, too, as an independent candidate.

Ross Perot surprised everyone by challenging both George Bush and Bill Clinton with interesting new ideas on how to run the country. Ross Perot got a lot of votes, but in the end, Bill Clinton won the election. Bill had promised to improve the economy, control government spending, and make it possible for all Americans to get better health care.

President Clinton celebrated by playing his saxophone on the night of his first inauguration.

President Clinton decided to put Hillary in charge of a committee to set up a new health-care system. Hillary set up her office in the White House near her husband's office. It was the first time a first lady had held such an important government job.

First Lady Hillary Clinton speaks to Congress during hearings on health-care reform.

Some people thought it was wrong for the president to give his wife a job like that one. When Hillary finished her plan, many felt it was too complicated. Some people worried that the new health-care system would allow the government to become involved in their personal medical decisions, too. The new health plan was never approved. It was a big disappointment for Bill and Hillary.

Bill Clinton was able to get a lot of other good things done, though. During his eight years as president, he signed some important bills into law. One gave employees the right to take time off of work to care for sick family members or new babies without getting in trouble with their bosses. President Clinton worked to improve trade between Mexico, the United States, and Canada. He helped stop the fighting during a bloody war in Kosovo, a region of Serbia in Eastern Europe.

President Clinton also helped the U.S. government balance its budget. For the first time in thirty years, the U.S. Treasury had money left over! Hardly anyone in Congress knew what to do with it.

Unfortunately, President Clinton was involved in a scandal during his presidency. In his second term, it was discovered that the president had an improper relationship with an office helper named Monica Lewinsky. When asked about it, the president was accused of lying under oath and trying to cover up information.

Lying under oath is known as perjury, which is a crime. Members of the House of Representatives agreed the president should be impeached, or tried, to determine if he had committed any crimes.

President Clinton sits quietly just before going on television on August 17, 1998. That night, he apologized to the American people for misleading them about his relationship with Monica Lewinsky.

The only other president to be impeached was Andrew Johnson in 1868. When a president is impeached, charges against him are brought before the Senate. Members of the Senate then decide if the president is guilty or not. In this case, the Senate voted against convicting President Clinton of any crimes.

Public service remained an important part of Bill Clinton's life after his presidency. In 2001, he went to India to help victims of an earthquake.

Many people felt what President Clinton did in his personal life was his own business. Others never forgave him. They believed the president should never lie, especially under oath. Overall, though, many people were happy with the way things went during Bill Clinton's presidency. There were lots of jobs, people's investments grew, and the U.S. government was making money.

Bill Clinton's second term ended in 2001, when he was fifty-four years old. He has kept very active in politics and has written a popular book about his life.